Morning Joy

Meditations for Those Who Have Suffered Loss

Helen Good Brenneman

HERALD PRESS
Scottdale, Pennsylvania
Kitchener, Ontario
1981

Library of Congress Cataloging in Publication Data

Brenneman, Helen Good.
  Morning joy.

  1. Consolation. I. Title.
BV4905.2.B68   242'.66   80-26449
ISBN 0-8361-1942-8 (pbk.)

MORNING JOY
Copyright © 1981 by Herald Press, Scottdale, PA 15683
  Published simultaneously in Canada by Herald Press,
  Kitchener, Ont. N2G 4M5
Library of Congress Catalog Card Number: 80-26449
International Standard Book Number: 0-8361-1942-8
Printed in the United States of America
Design: Alice B. Shetler
Cover Photo: H. Armstrong Roberts

81 82 83 84 85 86 10 9 8 7 6 5 4 3 2 1

To my former pastor,
John H. Mosemann,
who is unaware of his skill in
combining profundity with humility,
this book is gratefully dedicated.

Contents

Author's Preface 9

1. I Lie Down but I Do Not Sleep 13
   Our Guide, by Joseph R. Sizoo

2. A Cry in the Night 15
   From Day to Day, by Annie Johnson Flint

3. New Every Morning 17
   Great Is Thy Faithfulness, by Thomas O. Chisholm

4. Why Doesn't God Act? 19
   He Knows, by Grace Opperman

5. Blessings from Adversity 21
   Prayer for the Present Moment, by Lorie C. Gooding

6. A Word of Testimony 23
   From Fear unto Faith, by Clinton T. Howell

7. Hope for Hope 25
   Along the Road, by Robert Browning Hamilton

8. The Lonely Side of Grief 27
   Lonesome Valley (from the Southern Highlands)

9. Sources of Comfort 29
   We Share Abundantly (2 Corinthians 1:3-7)

10. As a Father Has Compassion 31
    Pass It On, Kurt Kaiser

11. Facing the Storm 33
    A Song of Praise (Psalm 95:1-7)

12. In Praise of Praise 35
    The Test of the Heart, by Ella Wheeler Wilcox

13. Witnessing in Adversity 37
    Supremely Happy (James 1:2-8; 12-13)

14. Pain, Our Teacher 39
    The Unwelcome Guest, by Grace Noll Crowell

15. In Praise of Tears 41
    My Refuge (Psalm 142)

16. A Daily Exercise 43
    A Thought (Author Unknown)

17. To Get Involved 45
    The Prayer of St. Francis of Assisi
18. The Upward Look 47
    My Faith Looks Up to Thee, by Ray Palmer
19. Get Rid of Worry 49
    I Never Knew a Night So Black, by John Kendrick Bangs
20. Healing for Broken Relationships 51
    His Forgiveness, by Corrie ten Boom
21. Trust. 53
    O Love That Wilt Not Let Me Go, by George Matheson
22. The Red-Sea Place 55
    Have No Fear (from Exodus 14)
23. Love Made Visible 57
    Sharing, by Maude V. Preston
24. Courage to Face Life 59
    Make Me Brave, by Grace Noll Crowell
25. Interdependence 61
    The Human Touch, Spencer Michael Free
26. A Happy Day 63
    Day by Day, by Julia Harris May
27. Looking for Answers 65
    I Look to Thee in Every Need, by Samuel Longfellow
28. Love's Tokens 67
    The Wages of Love (Author Unknown)
29. Godliness with Contentment 69
    I Needed the Quiet, by Alice Hansche Mortenson
30. Victorious Death 71
    Not as a Thief, by J. Paul Sauder
31. In Life and in Death. 73
    My Shepherd (Psalm 23)

Acknowledgments 75
The Author 77

Author's Preface

Morning Joy is a book of meditations for those who have suffered loss. There are many kinds of loss. A serious loss which has come to me is loss of health. A victim of multiple sclerosis for more than seventeen years, I am writing this book from my wheelchair in a nursing home.

I have often asked God for healing, have been anointed, and have experienced the laying on of hands. However, instead of granting healing, God has seen fit instead to enable me to live with the experience of longtime illness.

Many disadvantages are associated with the loss of one's health. With vision impaired, I am no longer able to read or to see the music so that I can play the piano. Long ago I needed to relinquish housekeeping duties to other members of the family. Each time I make my weekly visits home, I am newly aware that life can go on for them without my assistance.

In spite of my losses, God has enabled me to continue my writing. Seven of my nine books have been written since the onslaught of the disease. Probably I would not have taken time for writing had I been able to carry on my usual assignments, nor would I have had the inspiration and understandings upon which the books were built.

When I began writing this book I had not experienced the loss through death of any close family members. However, now that the manuscript is complete, both of my parents have died. Although they lived in another part of the country and I could not see them often, they were a great source of inspiration to me.

Perhaps the experience of grief is one of the least understood and loneliest crises of life. A highly individual matter, grief strikes in varied forms. One victim may have a completely different burden from another.

Those who wish to express sympathy are often puzzled what to say. They do not want to put salt instead of oil on the wounds of their friends. Fearing this, they make a regrettable mistake. They say nothing. Or, flustered by their need to say something, they answer questions their friends are not asking, or they utter inane comments off the tops of their heads.

The solution? I believe that we need simply to be there and sit silently as

Job's comforters did before we begin trying to play theologian and psychiatrist. We can show by the sense of touch a warmth of feeling that is meaningful to the mourner. We need to listen without reproof.

This book is an attempt to direct the thoughts of the reader to the God of hope, whatever loss is being experienced. The Christian hope is based on an explosive historical fact—the resurrection of Jesus Christ. We are to comfort one another with these words, and this book is an honest attempt to do this.

I want to thank Evelyn Bauer and the late Lydia Shank for helping me collect materials for this book. I especially express appreciation to the late Bertha Bender, without whose help the book would have been impossible. I also wish to thank Pat Roth and Verna Troyer for helping me go over the manuscript.

My prayer is that those who read this book and are suffering various kinds of loss may be inspired to make the most of the positive experiences which come out of their loss. I pray, too, that they may pass on to others what they have learned.

Helen Good Brenneman
Goshen, Indiana

Weeping may tarry for
the night, but joy comes
with the morning.

—*Psalm 30:5b*

Our Guide

The Bible speaks to the heart fresh every morning, for each new day and dilemma, and it satisfies the soul of the weary. The God who wrote His omnipotence against star clusters and Milky Ways, who wrote His painstaking care in the making of the simplest crustacean cells, also wrote His heart across the pages of this Book of Books. What a compass is to a pilot, what a song is to a weary heart, and what a latch is to a homeless wanderer, the Bible is to us—"a lamp unto our feet and a light upon our path."

There are many references to Abraham Lincoln's turning to the Bible for help and courage. At one time he said to a friend, "I have just finished reading on my knees the story of the Son of God in Gethsemane. I am in my Gethsemane now."

—*Joseph R. Sizoo*[1]

1

I Lie Down but I
Do Not Sleep

I lie down but I do not sleep.

Thoughts of the *past* drag by on leaden feet. Why did I not spend more time with my children when they were still at home? Why did I lose my cool that day? Why did I not pass on more love through physical touch? Why did I not pray more with my children and learn what they thought about prayer?

Thoughts of the *present* march by on business-directed feet. I have asked for strength for the day, but some days there does not seem to be enough fuel to power my engines. I am like a plane operating on one engine instead of four, trying to transport the cargo of a four-motor craft. There is not enough of me, O God, to accomplish my mission. I have been weighed in the balances and found wanting.

Thoughts of the *future* swirl by on panic-powered wings. O God, what if . . . I know there is a reaping for what has been sown. And there are trials sent for purifying your servants. But, O God, spare us the trials we cannot bear, as You have promised in Your Word. Keep us and those we love from physical danger and spiritual collapse. Make our final years serene with Your satisfaction and grace.

I lie down, but I do not sleep. I take my Source Book of guidance and wisdom from the shelf. Speak to me a word of comfort and hope, O God.

Spiritual Exercise:
Find words from the Bible which help you when you cannot sleep. Claim God's promise when he says in Psalm 4:8,

> "In peace I will both lie down and sleep;
> For thou alone, O Lord, makest me dwell in safety."

From Day to Day

My God will supply every need of yours.
—*Philippians 4:19*

Though we may weep the dark night through
Joy cometh with the morning's blue;
And though the day wears wearily,
Still, as our day our strength shall be;
When day draws on to shadowy night,
At eventide it shall be light.

When darkness folds us, calm and deep,
He giveth His beloved sleep;
Or if we wake and night seems long,
Then for our sighs He giveth song;
And when night yields to morning, then
Joy cometh with the dawn again.

—*Annie Johnson Flint*[2]

2

A Cry in the Night

I have always believed that every person should have goals and objectives despite the circumstances of one's life. Yet I was at a standstill with little to fill my days. A victim of multiple sclerosis, my vision had failed, and the work I loved at the typewriter was almost impossible. I wrote a few letters without proofreading them. Other work was also difficult, as coordination and strength were on the decrease. Communication with persons, even those I loved best, was sometimes difficult. It seems one needs to be active to have something to talk about.

Some people think that the words, "The Lord helps those who help themselves," are in the Bible. Instead, there are verses such as "He gives power to the faint, and to him who has no might he increases strength" (Isaiah 40:29).

Fortunately, when we realize our weakness, we can maximize God's loving-kindness and enabling grace. Thus in our weakness God is made strong.

Spiritual Exercise:
Make two lists:

one, of the circumstances in your life which are difficult; the other, possible solutions which your faith brings to your mind.

Great Is Thy Faithfulness

Great is Thy faithfulness, O God my Father,
There is no shadow of turning with Thee;
Thou changest not, Thy compassions, they fail not;
As Thou hast been Thou forever wilt be.

Refrain:
Great is Thy faithfulness! Great is Thy faithfulness!
Morning by morning new mercies I see;
All I have needed Thy hand hath provided.
Great is Thy faithfulness! Lord unto me!

Summer and winter, and springtime and harvest,
Sun, moon, and stars in their courses above,
Join with all nature in manifold witness
To Thy great faithfulness, mercy, and love.

Pardon for sin and a peace that endureth,
Thy own dear presence to cheer and to guide;
Strength for today and bright hope for tomorrow,
Blessings all mine, with ten thousand beside!

—Thomas O. Chisholm

3

New Every Morning

"When I lost my wife," an aged gentleman confided, "my life was like a tree struck by lightning, right down through the trunk."

The death of a loved one is a great loss, perhaps life's greatest. It is losing part of one's own person, part of one's very being. But there are other losses: disappointments, spiritual crises, unexpected tragedies, sometimes the diminishment of personhood, the loss of life's goals and purposes, shock, and perhaps a temporary imbalance. One may lose a limb, one's general health, a good job, a precious possession, or the love and respect of a friend.

One mother, contemplated what had befallen her family and, in the midst of deep pain, claimed God's real presence and help. She wrote:

NEW EVERY MORNING

Family sorrow. New every morning as I awake to harsh reality. Crushing afresh after each soothing sleep . . . is it really true? Why did this have to happen to us? . . . How can I bear this grief . . . ?

Comfort. New every morning. Still no answers to the mysteries of suffering, yet strength for the day. Faith in God and his purpose when all seems hopeless and I am at the end of myself. Trusting God as a child does his father while walking in the dark. Sensing the presence of the Person who will never leave me nor forsake me. His love, mercy, and faithfulness are new every morning.

It's just as the Bible says, "The steadfast love of the Lord never ceases, his mercies never come to an end; they are new every morning; great is thy faithfulness."[3]

Spiritual Exercise:

Meditate on the hymn on the opposite page. Look for an opportunity to share God's faithfulness today.

He Knows

I do not know what lies ahead,
I only know that He hath said
That he will never leave alone
The blood-bought ones, who are His own.

I do not know the way to take,
I only know that He will make
Each step, His way, and go before;
I need not fear. His way is sure.

I do not always understand
His ways; but this I need to know:
I only know He holds my hand
And where He leads me, I will go.

—Grace Opperman[4]

4

Why Doesn't God Act?

God speaks through personal tragedy. But deep suffering often precedes the Word of God. Some prayers are so intense that only a cry goes up to God. Here are a few short prayers which, "uttered or unexpressed," rise from the lips of one who is suffering:

O God, HELP!

The thing that I feared has come upon me, and what I dread befalls me. This thing—it is too much for me—I can't cope with the facts! It is a problem without a solution. O God, don't You care that I perish?

O God, NO!

No, this thing cannot happen to me! It is the kind of thing which you read about in the newspaper—that happens to someone else in a distant state, or the cousin of your friend. It can't happen to me, to us! I simply will not believe it. It was not in the plans for my life.

O God, WHY?

Give me a reason, just give me one reason, God! It doesn't make sense. What did I do to deserve this? Am I worse than others that You need to discipline me in this way? Am I a terrible sinner? What possible good can come out of this mess?

O God, HOW LONG?

O God, if You are so great, if You have all that power, then why don't You do something about all this? Are You sleeping, or have You forgotten me altogether? Surely You are not dead, but the silence from heaven is more than I can bear. How long, how long, O God, until You act in my behalf?

But, hopefully, the sufferer moves beyond the stage of "Listen, Lord, Thy servant speaketh," important as this stage is to his ultimate healing. When, in quietness he is able to say, "Speak, Lord; for thy servant heareth," there comes a word of courage and hope: "Be still, and know that I am God. . . . Lo, I am with you. . . . My grace is sufficient for you, for my power is made perfect in weakness. . . ." Nothing "will be able to separate [you] . . . from the love of God, in Christ Jesus our Lord."

And, in answer to the still, small voice, the sufferer is able to pray: "Oh, God, YES! I had heard of thee by the hearing of the ear, but now my eye sees thee."

Spiritual Exercise:

Reread "He Knows" on the opposite page and close your meditation with the prayer, "Speak, Lord; for thy servant heareth."

Prayer for the Present Moment

They that wait upon the Lord—
Oh, yes, I know,
shall feel their strength returning,
by and by
shall rise from prayer to walk—
to run—to fly.
The loving-kindness of the Lord is great
to those who wait.

But, Lord,
my need is now,
as near as sunrise. With the light tomorrow
I must have strength to bear the load again,
calm courage in the face of present sorrow,
and wisdom as I walk this maze of pain.
These things I ask of Thee,
that I fail not those hearts that lean on me.
Let Thy dear presence be
my stay, and let Thy mercies be as great
to one who cannot wait.

—Lorie C. Gooding[5]

5

Blessings From Adversity

A pearl is a temple built around a grain of sand.
—Kahlil Gibran

We know that sand inside an oyster is an irritant, but as a result of its being there a pearl is formed. Likewise conditions which may seem irritating often form pearls in our lives.

A couple whose child needed hospitalization for a nervous disorder were forced, because of the circumstances, to look at their marriage. As a result, they grew closer in their relationship to each other.

The important question which we must ask ourselves when difficulty comes is, "What does God want to teach me through this problem?"

An aged gentleman, too old to have a cataract operation, said, "I wonder what God has to teach me through blindness."

If we look at all our adversities in this manner we will find some good in every situation.

Spiritual Exercise:
Ask God what He has to teach you through your present circumstances. Then ask Him in this adversity to form a pearl around the sand of your difficulty.

From Fear unto Faith

Father, do Thou this day free me—
    From fear of the future;
    From anxiety for the morrow;
    From bitterness toward anyone;
    From cowardice in face of danger;
    From laziness in face of work;
    From failure before opportunity;
    From weakness when Thy power is at hand.

But fill me, I beseech Thee, with—
    Love that knows no barriers;
    Courage that cannot be shaken;
    Faith strong enough for the darkness;
    Strength sufficient for my tasks;
    Loyalty to Thy kingdom's goal;
    Wisdom to meet life's complexities;
    Grace to meet life's perplexities;
    Power to lift men unto Thee.

—Clinton T. Howell[6]

6

A Word of Testimony

A young girl, Jill Liechty, who knew she was facing death, wrote the following letter:

Dear Friends:

I feel the need to express thanks and appreciation to you loving people for the way you have supported me and my family. You all have shown Christ's love to myself and my family in your response to us. It's wonderful to be in a caring community.

During my second surgery I was surrounded by many fine doctors and nurses. In spite of all the knowledge granted to man they were unable to offer hope for my physical body.

My hope, therefore, is in God's perfect will. He has granted me the gift of peace concerning life and death. I truly feel as Paul did in Philippians 1.20, 21, LB. "For I live in eager expectations and hope that I will never do anything that will cause me to be ashamed of myself but that I will always be ready to speak out boldly for Christ while I am going through all these trials here, just as I have in the past, and that I will always be an honor to Christ, whether I live or whether I must die. For to me, living means opportunities for Christ, and dying—well, that's better yet!"

I don't believe that I am anyone special. Christ will come to you in the same way He has shown Himself to me. He has given me perfect peace and the assurance of a life far greater than the life we have here. As you have been praying for me I'm certain that God is blessing you. My continual prayer for all of you is if you do not know Christ, that somehow, someday, He will speak to your heart as He did to mine years ago.

If God doesn't heal me, I'll see you in heaven!

Jill [7]

Spiritual Exercise:

Pray a silent prayer in which you hold up to God your soul's deepest need. Then pray a prayer of thanksgiving for the blessings of your day.

Along the Road

I walked a mile with Pleasure;
   She chattered all the way,
But left me none the wiser
   For all she had to say.

I walked a mile with Sorrow
   And ne'er a word said she;
But oh, the things I learned from her
   When Sorrow walked with me!

—Robert Browning Hamilton[8]

7

Hope for Hope

When Hope was a little girl, she was sometimes teased about her name. "Perhaps," she was told, "you are hoping for a Christmas gift, or special guests at a family picnic."

Now that she is grown, Hope's name has added significance for her. Since she is a Christian, Hope realizes that there is a "Christian hope." This became especially clear to her when her mother died. Hope is hoping for the day when she will be reunited with her mother. It gives her pleasure to realize that the very one who gave her her name reminded her of the joyous reunion to come.

"If for this life only we have hoped in Christ, we are of all men most to be pitied" (1 Corinthians 15:19).

"But we would not have you ignorant, brethren, concerning those who are asleep, that you may not grieve as others do who have no hope" (1 Thessalonians 4:13).

Paul does not tell us it is wrong to sorrow. Sorrow is a normal emotion which comes from many of life's circumstances. But, as in the case of those of whom he speaks—the bereaved—sorrow is accompanied by hope. This hope brings courage, a courage which makes it possible to share with others.

Let us pray that God will sanctify our sorrow so that we will be better able to understand the sorrow of a friend.

Let the truth of the resurrection be a healing experience in your life.

Benediction:

And may the God of hope fill you with all joy and peace by your faith in him, until, by the power of the Holy Spirit, you overflow with hope. Romans 15:13, NEB.

Lonesome Valley

Jesus walked this lonesome valley,
He had to walk it by Himself;
Oh, nobody else could walk it for Him—
He had to walk it by Himself.

We must walk this lonesome valley;
We have to walk it by ourselves;
Oh, nobody else can walk it for us—
We have to walk it by ourselves.

—From the Southern Highlands

8

The Lonely Side of Grief

Although we bear each other's burdens and share each other's griefs, there is an aloneness in the experience of grief, a solitude which in a way makes it a private affair.

"After my husband's death," a widow said, "people often told me that now I would be in a better position to sympathize with others. I'm not so sure. It seems to me that grief is such an individual matter—no one really understands just how another person feels."

Maybe we shouldn't try.

"After my fiancé was taken in an accident," one young woman shared, "people kept coming to me and telling me how I *ought* to feel. But I didn't feel that way. What I needed was someone to sit and listen to how I *really* felt."

There are times when we have to work out our own salvation, so to speak, in our own company. There are struggles which no other human being can help us solve. As a Japanese mother once said, "Sometimes I have to go apart to organize my thoughts."

Jacob had to wrestle with his angel alone, even though his wives, children, and servants were not far away. The prophet Elijah had to retreat to his mountain cave before he was ready to hear the still, small voice of God and to understand that he was not alone in his spiritual convictions.

Even Jesus, when facing the excruciating ordeal of a painful death and bearing the sins and burdens of the whole world, had to find a sheltered spot in a midnight garden to sweat out His agony. But He wanted His intimate friends to be within earshot; He needed their moral support and their prayers. The spiritual on the opposite page tells it as it was.

We, too, must walk our lonesome valleys, valleys of innermost need, shock, adjustment, confession, forsakenness, of struggle against self-pity and despair, of decision-making.

But, to our surprise, as we seem to be all alone walking through our valley, conscious of the quietness of the night and the noise of our own heartbeat, suddenly we feel a touch on our shoulder and we are aware of a Presence. He was there all the time! We don't have to explain anything to Him, for He understands. He walked this path before we did.

Benediction:
Stand tall and go through the new day knowing that you are not really alone. Practice the presence of God.

We Share Abundantly

Blessed be the God and Father of our Lord Jesus Christ, the Father of mercies and God of all comfort, who comforts us in all our affliction, so that we may be able to comfort those who are in any affliction, with the comfort with which we ourselves are comforted by God. For as we share abundantly in Christ's sufferings, so through Christ we share abundantly in comfort too. If we are afflicted, it is for your comfort and salvation; and if we are comforted, it is for your comfort, which you experience when you patiently endure the same sufferings that we suffer. Our hope for you is unshaken; for we know that as you share in our sufferings, you will also share in our comfort.

—2 Corinthians 1:3-7

9

Sources of Comfort

Blessed are those who mourn: for they shall be comforted.
—*Matthew 5:4*

If we were to read only the first part of this verse, many questions would present themselves. It seems paradoxical that mourners should be happy, but the beatitude goes on to explain that the mourner is comforted.

Comfort comes in unexpected ways. We may have had a good day or have experienced comfort without knowing why, only later learning that someone was praying for us. Other sources of comfort include the spontaneous affection of a little child, the squeeze of a warm handshake, a visit from a good friend, remembering words of encouragement, or an apt quotation once recorded in our memory.

The Holy Spirit, the ever-present gift of God, is the greatest source of comfort to the Christian.

We are blessed when we mourn because comfort comes our way—a comfort which we experience but find difficult to verbalize.

Benediction:

May the God of comfort bring promise to your day and may you experience the warmth of His presence and hope.

Pass It On

It only takes a spark to get a fire going,
And soon all those around can warm up to its glowing.
That's how it is with God's love:
Once you've experienced it
You spread His love to everyone—
You want to pass it on.

What a wondrous time is spring when all the trees are budding!
The birds begin to sing, the flowers start their blooming.
That's how it is with God's love, once you've experienced it
You want to sing, it's fresh like spring,
You want to pass it on.

I wish for you, my friend, this happiness that I've found.
You can depend on Him, it matters not where you're bound.
I'll shout it from the mountaintop—I want my world to know
The Lord of love has come to me, I want to pass it on.

—Kurt Kaiser

10

As a Father Has Compassion

A minister-father who had recently moved from one location to another tells this story about his tiny daughter, who felt a bit unsettled. When she whimpered late one night, he went into her room to comfort her. Taking his hand she laid it on her little bottom and said only one word, "pat." She needed the touch of a hand from a father she knew she could trust.

Another father was widowed and left with a family of nine children. Trying to double as both father and mother, he found himself helping his eldest to cook the meals, supervising the cleaning, ineptly braiding snarled hair, and moonlighting at part-time jobs to meet the family bills. One of his daughters, now a grandmother herself, remembers how her father tried to satisfy the emotional needs of his younger children, taking them two-by-two to the rocker, and singing lullabies until the little ones fell asleep.

When one has been the recipient of such love, it is not hard to trust a heavenly Father, who has asked us to address Him with the intimate term, "Abba, Father." This love must be passed on. On the day of my youngest daughter's baptism, she and some of her high school friends sang the song "Pass It On" as a witness to their understanding of God's love.

That's how it is with God's love once you've experienced it, you want to pass it on.

Spiritual Exercise:
Think of something that has blessed your life during the past week. Try to pass this on to someone today.

A Song of Praise

Come, let us praise the Lord!
Let us sing for joy to God, who protects us!
Let us come before him with thanksgiving
    and sing joyful songs of praise.
For the Lord is a mighty God,
    a mighty king over all the gods.
He rules over the whole earth,
    from the deepest caves to the highest hills.
He rules over the sea, which he made;
    the land also, which he himself formed.

Come, let us bow down and worship him;
    let us kneel before the Lord, our Maker!
He is our God;
    we are the people he cares for,
    the flock for which he provides.

—Psalm 95:1-7, TEV

11

Facing the Storm

Many people facing adversity thank God that things are not worse than they are. This seems like a rather negative way of praising God. The Apostle Paul writes, "The Lord is near; have no anxiety, but in everything make your requests known to God in prayer and petition with thanksgiving. Then the peace of God, which is beyond our utmost understanding, will keep guard over your hearts and your thoughts, in Christ Jesus" (Philippians 4:6-7, NEB). This seems like a more positive way to thank God.

This also should protect us from prayers that are always begging but never thanking.

It is certainly not wrong for us to come to our heavenly Parent with requests, be they ever so small, but our faith is strengthened when we think of the bountiful blessings that God has already bestowed on us.

Spiritual Exercise:

Pray a prayer of thanksgiving in which you ask for nothing, but praise God for everything. During your daily routine look for things for which to praise.

The Test of the Heart

It is easy enough to be pleasant
   When life flows by like a song,
But the man worthwhile is one who will smile
   When everything goes dead wrong.
For the test of the heart is trouble,
   And it always comes with the years,
And the smile that is worth the praises of earth
   Is the smile that shines through tears.

—Ella Wheeler Wilcox[9]

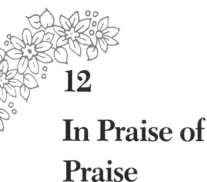

12

In Praise of Praise

Let everything that breathes praise the Lord!

—Psalm 150:6

A teacher friend decided to take her second-grade class to visit a large turkey farm.

One small boy who had difficulty learning the academic rudiments observed the several thousand turkeys and exclaimed,

"Why, they're saying, 'Hallelujah!' "

"Is that what they're saying, Willie?" his teacher asked.

"Yes! Don't you hear? They're saying, 'Hallelujah!' " The child insisted, and his teacher wondered if it took such a child to hear what perhaps many of God's creatures are saying. For does not the Bible say that everything that breathes should praise the Lord?

When we praise God for His goodness, we join the mighty "Hallelujah Chorus" of the universe. It is not hard to praise God when things are going our way, but in the loss of friendship, of loved ones, of prestige, of security, and health comes the test of our faith. Faith is believing in a force that is all good and all love in spite of life's circumstances. It is believing in a personal, loving Father when we assent but cannot see. Whether we verbalize this faith in words of praise or simply live thankful, God-honoring lives, we show by our attitudes whether we are among those who join in praising God for life and life's ventures.

Spiritual Exercise:

Think of an experience in your life where all things have worked together for good. Turn your *present* circumstances over to God.

Supremely Happy

My brothers, whenever you have to face trials of many
kinds, count yourselves supremely happy, in the knowledge
that such testing of your faith breeds fortitude, and if you give
fortitude full play you will go on to complete a balanced
character that will fall short in nothing. If any of you falls short
in wisdom, he should ask God for it and it will be given him,
for God is a generous giver who neither refuses nor reproaches
anyone. But he must ask in faith, without a doubt in his mind;
for the doubter is like a heaving sea ruffled by the wind. A
man of that kind must not expect the Lord to give him
anything; he is double-minded, and never can keep a steady
course.

Happy the man who remains steadfast under trial, for
having passed that test he will receive for his prize the gift of
life promised to those who love God. No one under trial or
temptation should say, "I am being tempted by God"; for God
is untouched by evil, and does not himself tempt anyone.

—James 1:2-8; 12-13, NEB

13

Witnessing in Adversity

Samuel Shoemaker tells of one of the greatest saints he ever knew. An old lady in New York was struck by a tire which flew off a passing truck and broke one of her hips. She was in the hospital in great pain and yet said with a smile, "Well, I wonder what God has for me to do here!" On her back she could not read her Bible, so she asked her nurse to read it to her. The nurse was a skeptic at first, but not when she left. The radiance which she saw reflected from this lady's face changed her.

If we truly believe that God has a pattern for our lives, we will, like this Christian woman, see each circumstance as part of the pattern. But when this circumstance arises, we need to remind ourselves of our original commitment and God's purpose for us. Probably the greatest opportunities for witness to others come at times of adversity. Sometimes we do not think of this as a witness, but there are always persons who observe us as we face trial. It is enough that we remain faithful.

Spiritual Exercise:

Think of the hardest experience that you have had to face. Ask God to show you how you can use this experience for personal growth and witness to others.

The Unwelcome Guest

Pain stayed so long I said to him today,
"I will not have you with me anymore."
I stamped my foot and said, "Be on your way,"
And then paused, startled at the look he wore.
"I who am your friend," he said to me,
"I who am your teacher—all you know
Of understanding love and sympathy
And patience I have taught you, shall I go?"

He spoke the truth, this strange unwelcome guest.
I watched him leave, and knew his way was wise.
He left a heart grown tender in my breast.
He left a far, clear vision in my eyes.
I dried my tears and lifted up a song
Even for one who tortured me so long.

—*Grace Noll Crowell*

From *Comfort Ye My People* by Grace Noll Crowell (Nashville, Tenn.: The Upper Room, 1945), p. 14. Used by permission of the publisher.

14

Pain, Our Teacher

All of us live with some circumstances that we would not choose for ourselves. A missionary to Uruguay, Daniel Miller, was arrested unjustly one day and subjected to a great deal of torture. He was slapped, kicked, given electric shock, and made to stand all day with his feet apart and his hands held high.

Later he wrote to his home office:

> The experience was personally very meaningful. For meditation during Holy Week I believe an army barracks beats a monastery! I missed three days of our congregational retreat, but by some incredible scheduling the army jeep delivered me to the church door just as they were beginning the Holy Thursday worship service consisting of a torchlight dramatization of Holy Week. I was carried immediately from the barracks where I had been meditating on Christ in that situation to the barracks that the church had created to relive Christ's experience! Holy Week has meant more to me this year than ever before in my life.

Most of our trials may not be as dramatic as Daniel Miller's, but the same resources are ours.

Spiritual Exercise:

Read the poem on the opposite page. What have you learned from adversity in your own life? Can you think of painful situations you have experienced that have taught you lessons?

My Refuge

I cry with my voice to the Lord,
    with my voice I make my supplication to the Lord,
I pour out my complaint before him,
    I tell my trouble before him.
When my spirit is faint,
    thou knowest my way!

In the path where I walk
    they have hidden a trap for me.
I look to the right and watch,
    but there is none who takes notice of me;
no refuge remains to me,
    no man cares for me.

I cry to thee, O Lord;
    I say, Thou art my refuge,
    my portion in the land of the living.
Give heed to my cry;
    for I am brought very low!

Deliver me from my persecutors;
    for they are too strong for me!
Bring me out of prison,
    that I may give thanks to thy name!
The righteous will surround me;
    for thou wilt deal bountifully with me.

(Prayed while David was hiding in the cave
    when King Saul was pursuing him.)

—Psalm 142

15

In Praise of Tears

I remember the time a child was asked to recite a Scripture verse by memory but was unprepared. Triumphantly he said, "Jesus wept" (John 11:35). Little did he realize what he was saying. For although this is the shortest verse in the Bible, it is one of the most profound.

One seldom sees a strong man cry, for boys are conditioned early in life to believe that restraint is a masculine characteristic. Yet a quick glance in a Bible concordance shows that Jesus was not the only man who shed tears in public. In times of crisis Esau, Jacob, David, Jonathan, Saul, Joash, Hezekiah, Job, Peter, and Nehemiah all cried. Emotion was not despised or hidden in Bible times.

Jesus cried on more than one occasion. We know that He was moved to tears one day as He sat on a hill overlooking Jerusalem. He sobbed, "Jerusalem, Jerusalem! You kill the prophets, you stone the messengers God has sent you! How many times I wanted to put my arms around all your people, just as a hen gathers her chicks under her wings, but you would not let me!" (Luke 13:34, TEV).

The eleventh chapter of John tells of Jesus' going to the tomb of Lazarus, His close friend who had died. When Mary and Martha learned that Jesus was near, they cried out, "If You had been here, our brother would not have died."

When Jesus saw Mary's tears and the tears of her friends, He also broke down and cried. He cried because He cared about people. He had concern for heartaches, disappointments, frustrations, and bewilderments of individuals. He identified with persons, put Himself in their shoes, sat where they sat, felt for them, and responded to their needs. He possessed that quality so much needed by parents, friends, authors, artists, teachers, anyone—empathy, the ability to put oneself in another person's place.

Jesus sympathized, but He also empathized. He exemplified that quality encouraged by the Apostle Paul in Romans 12:15: "Be happy with those who are happy, weep with those who weep" (TEV). And we are told that He has never stopped caring, that we are to cast our care upon Him, for He cares for us.

Benediction:
May the God of all comfort be your joy even though tears may be part of your experience. Is there someone with whom *you* can empathize today?

A Thought

I know not why
There comes to me today
The thought of someone
Miles and miles away
Unless there be a need
That I should pray.

—*Author Unknown*

16

A Daily Exercise

A riddle in life might be, "What can we do at the same time that we are doing something else?" The answer, of course, is *pray*. More specifically, let us think of intercessory prayer, prayer for the needs of others. This we can do despite crippling circumstances of our own.

At the same time that we are doing daily routine chores we can hold up to God those whom we love. We do not always know the needs of our friends, but God knows.

We are told in Philippians 1:3, "I thank my God in all my remembrance of you." In other words, just the thought of someone can stimulate a prayer for him. We can thank God for his life, pray for his needs, and ask God's blessing on his day. This prayer does not take eloquence, but just a concern and love for a friend. Perhaps praying such a prayer can help us to a deeper love for others.

Benediction:
Intercede for someone you know and love. Ask a specific blessing or benediction on his day.

The Prayer of St. Francis of Assisi

Lord, make me an instrument of Thy peace;
Where there is hatred, let me sow love;
Where there is injury, pardon;
Where there is doubt, faith;
Where there is despair, hope;
Where there is darkness, light; and
Where there is sadness, joy.
Divine Master,
Grant that I may not so much seek to be
Consoled as to console;
To be understood as to understand;
To be loved as to love;
For it is in giving that we receive;
It is in pardoning that we are pardoned;
And it is in dying that we are born to eternal life.

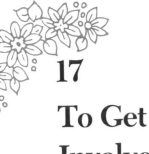

17

To Get Involved

A friend of ours, a former student at a nearby college who went on to Princeton and became a man of great influence, was known for his love for people. While he was at Princeton he sometimes put on old clothes, sat on the curb with his arms around a transient, and talked of the love of God.

That is what Jesus Christ did. He put on our old clothes of flesh, sat down on the curb of our battered world, put His arms around us, and said, "For God so loved the world that he gave his only Son, that whoever believes in him should not perish but have eternal life" (John 3:16).

When mothers brought their children to sit on His lap, His busy disciples would have shuttled them away, but He said, "Stop! These children are special with the Father. They are people. I have time for children."

When He attended a party with sinners, His shocked friends exclaimed, "Dear, dear!" But He said, "Don't you understand yet that I came into the world to save sinners, not goody-goodies? I came to serve the sick, the brokenhearted, the down-and-outers, and the up-and-outers. I came to get involved with people—all kinds of people. I came to do the will of my Father, who is love."

Spiritul Exercise:

Ask God to give you love like Christ's for people of all kinds and ages. Ask Him to help someone who needs a friend to cross your path today. If no one comes to you, ask for guidance in seeking out such a person.

My Faith Looks Up to Thee

My faith looks up to Thee, Thou Lamb of Calvary,
Savior divine: now hear me while I pray,
Take all my guilt away, O let me from this day
Be wholly Thine.

May Thy rich grace impart strength to my fainting heart,
My zeal inspire; as Thou hast died for me,
O may my love to Thee, pure, warm, and changeless be,
A living fire.

While life's dark maze I tread, and griefs around me spread,
Be Thou my guide; bid darkness turn to day,
Wipe sorrow's tears away, nor let me ever stray
From Thee aside.

When ends life's transient dream, when death's cold, sullen stream
Shall o'er me roll, blest Savior, then, in love,
Fear and distrust remove; O bear me safe above,
A ransomed soul.

—Ray Palmer

18

The Upward Look

A friend tells me that when she was in Copenhagen she saw Thorvaldsen's life-sized statue of Christ standing with head bowed and arms outstretched. She was told that to get the best look at His face, one had to kneel and look up. However, there was no place provided to do this. But later, in the Mormon center in Salt Lake City, she saw a replica of this statue and had the privilege of kneeling before it and looking up. It was true. From this position she saw the beauty of His compassionate face looking down upon her.

> If you want to be miserable, look inside.
> If you want to be distracted, look around.
> If you want to be peaceful, look up.
> —Author unknown

When we are tempted to pity ourselves, it is time for the upward look. When we look up, we get a glimpse of the God who loves us. And we remember that He has goals and purposes for our lives that are not always visible.

Spiritual Exercise:

Sing the song on the opposite page. Take time this morning for the upward look. Thank God for His loving presence and ask Him to reveal His purposes for your day.

I Never Knew a Night So Black

I never knew a night so black
Light failed to follow in its track.
I never knew a storm so gray
It failed to have its clearing day.
I never knew such black despair
That there was not a rift somewhere.
I never knew an hour so drear
Love could not fill it full of cheer.

—*John Kendrick Bangs*[10]

19

Get Rid of Worry

Worry is like sitting in a rocking chair: it keeps you busy but it gets you nowhere.

—Author Unknown

A wife, speaking of her husband, said, "I do his worrying for him." Most of us do our worrying for ourselves, and most of us can testify that it gets us nowhere.

What can we substitute for worry in ridding our lives of this menace? A strong faith, to be sure, is the best substitute. We know that God, who loves us more than anyone else, is taking care of us and our loved ones. The daily habit of talking things over with Him is the positive way of getting rid of worry.

Spiritual Exercise:

Think of the things which cause you to worry. Some may be the result of an overactive imagination, but many may be based on real situations. Talk these over with your heavenly Father. What positive actions might He inspire in you in place of worry?

His Forgiveness

Corrie ten Boom, who, with her sister Betsie, had suffered excruciatingly while in concentration camps, tells the following story in the book *The Hiding Place:*[11]

It was at a church service in Munich that I saw him, the former S.S. man who had stood guard at the shower-room door in the processing center at Ravensbruck. He was the first of our actual jailers that I had seen since that time. And suddenly it was all there—the roomful of mocking men, the heaps of clothing, Betsie's pain-blanched face.

He came up to me as the church was emptying, beaming and bowing. "How grateful I am for your message, *Fraulein,*" he said. "To think that, as you say, He has washed my sins away!"

His hand was thrust out to shake mine. And I, who had preached so often to the people in Bloemendaal the need to forgive, kept my hand at my side.

Even as the angry, vengeful thoughts boiled through me, I saw the sin of them. Jesus Christ had died for this man; was I going to ask for more? "Lord Jesus," I prayed, "forgive me and help me to forgive him."

I tried to smile, I struggled to raise my hand. I could not. I felt nothing, not the slightest spark of warmth or charity. And so again I breathed a silent prayer. "Jesus, I cannot forgive him. Give me Your forgiveness."

As I took his hand the most incredible thing happened. From my shoulder along my arm and through my hand a current seemed to pass from me to him, while into my heart sprang a love for this stranger that almost overwhelmed me.

And so I discovered that it is not on our forgiveness any more than on our goodness that the world's healing hinges, but on His. When He tells us to love our enemies, He gives, along with the command, the love itself.

20

Healing for Broken Relationships

On the March sheet of a calendar one year was the following quotation: "The sages do not consider that making no mistakes is a blessing. They believe that the great virtue of man lies in his ability to correct his mistakes and continually to make a new man of himself."

One of the greatest losses which we can experience is the breaking of personal relationships. These may be anything from a broken friendship to the severing of the deep relationship of marriage. All broken relationships are filled with trauma. Even the young who terminate relationships suffer from the experience.

A friend, learning that I was writing a book for those suffering loss, said, "Don't forget to mention divorce. It is a living death. I know, for I have experienced it." Marriage, being a lifetime commitment, is fraught with intense suffering when separation or divorce occurs.

In any case, when reconciliation takes place, what we seek to experience is healing, and healing comes only from God. Of course, we have a part to play in it, for we must put ourselves in the position of being healed and of being a healing force. Restored relationships follow forgiveness and love.

Spiritual Exercise:

Is there any relationship in our life which is broken or is strained by ill will or misunderstanding? Ask God's guidance and take some steps today toward a healing of the relationships. Pray the Lord's Prayer, noticing how God's forgiveness is dependent on our forgiveness of others.

O Love That Wilt Not Let Me Go

O love that wilt not let me go,
I rest my weary soul in Thee;
I give Thee back the life I owe,
That in Thine ocean depths its flow
May richer, fuller be.

O light that follow'st all my way,
I yield my flick'ring torch to Thee;
My heart restores its borrowed ray,
That in Thy sunshine's blaze its day
May brighter, fairer be.

O joy that seekest me through pain,
I cannot close my heart to Thee;
I trace the rainbow through the rain,
And feel the promise is not vain
That morn shall tearless be.

O cross that liftest up my head,
I dare not ask to fly from Thee;
I lay in dust life's glory dead,
And from the ground there blossoms red
Life that shall endless be. Amen.

—George Matheson

21

Trust

Indeed I count everything as loss because of the surpassing worth of knowing Christ Jesus my Lord. For his sake I have suffered the loss of all things, and count them as refuse, in order that I may gain Christ.

—Philippians 3:8

The Apostle Paul reminds us that it is only too easy to trust in wrong things. We must come to the place where we are ready to throw out all our pet philosophies for the eternal verities of a Christian life determined to be totally dependent on Christ.

When we experience real loss, we have the choice of several types of response. We can indulge in self-pity, we can blame God, or we can do as the Apostle Paul suggests—consider these things as expendable and count them as loss for Christ. When we view all the circumstances of our lives as dependent on the Lord who loves us, we can face whatever comes with courage.

Spiritual Exercise:

Make a list of things in which we are tempted to trust in contrast to the real and genuine marks of faith.

Benediction:

May God, who knows you better than you know yourself, lead you through this day and bless your efforts to accomplish much for His kingdom. May you relax, trusting His providence.

Have No Fear

You may wish to read the entire chapter of Exodus 14 to refresh your mind for the setting of today's meditation. In brief it is as follows:

The children of Israel were fleeing from cruel King Pharaoh of Egypt, whose army was pursuing them to force them to return to Egypt. They found to their terror that they were trapped with the Red Sea in front of them and the Egyptian army behind them in hot pursuit. Desperately they cried out to Moses.

"Have no fear," Moses answered; "stand firm and see the deliverance that the Lord will bring you this day; for as sure as you see the Egyptians now, you will never see them again. The Lord will fight for you; so hold your peace."

The Lord said to Moses . . . "Tell the Israelites to strike camp. And you shall raise high your staff, stretch out your hand over the sea and cleave it in two, so that the Israelites can pass through the sea on dry ground. . . ."

Then Moses stretched out his hand over the sea, and the Lord drove the sea away all night with a strong east wind and turned the sea-bed into dry land. The waters were torn apart, and the Israelites went through the sea on the dry ground, while the waters made a wall for them to right and to left.

—Excerpts from Exodus 14, NEB

22

The Red-Sea Place

Sooner or later all of us come to the "Red-Sea Place" in life.

—*Dorothea S. Kopplin*

THE RED-SEA PLACE

Have you come to the *Red-Sea Place* in your life,
Where, in spite of all you can do,
There is no way out, there is no way back,
There is no other way but—through?

Then wait on the Lord with trust serene,
Till the night of fear is gone;
He will send the wind, He will keep the floods,
When He says to your soul, "Go on."

—*Annie Johnson Flint*[12]

Dorothea S. Kopplin, author of the book *Something to Live By*, learned that she might not have long to live. This inspired her to put together this book of quotations for her children. Mrs. Kopplin was a good example of someone who followed the advice of the above poem. Facing the *Red-Sea Place* in her life, she stepped forth "on dry ground."

If the children of Israel had not been willing to step forth in faith, the miracle of the dry land would not have done them any good. We too must be willing to take the steps of faith which will take us to the other side. Perhaps we may be tempted to test God's providence by stepping in with one toe. But when God wants to make a miracle for us, we have only to cooperate in faith and make it ours.

Spiritual Exercise:
THINK! Is there a *Red-Sea Place* in your life through which you dread to take a step? Ask God for faith that He will give you a path of dry land over which you may pass this day.

Sharing

There isn't much that I can do, but I can
share my bread with you, and I can share
my joy with you, and sometimes share a
sorrow, too . . . as on our way we go.

There isn't much that I can do, but I can
sit an hour with you, and I can share
a joke with you, and sometimes share
reverses, too . . . as on our way we go.

There isn't much that I can do, but I can
share my flowers with you, and I can
share my books with you, and sometimes share your
burdens, too . . . as on our way we go.

There isn't much that I can do, but I can
share my songs with you, and I can share
my mirth with you, and sometimes come and
laugh with you . . . as on our way we go.

There isn't much that I can do, but I can
share my hopes with you, and I can share my
fears with you, and sometimes shed some
tears with you . . . as on our way we go.

There isn't much that I can do, but I can
share my friends with you, and I can share
my life with you, and ofttimes share a
prayer with you . . . as on our way we go.

—Maude V. Preston[13]

23

Love Made Visible

Children who are assigned daily chores do not always think of them as blessings, but as we grow older we realize that there is a "miracle" in the daily routine. This value can be lost if work is misused, such as when a person allows work to keep him from facing important decisions or blind him to the needs of others. The misuse of work can be illustrated by the person who is so busy that he fails to answer the questions of a little child, or to share the heartache of a suffering friend.

Strange as it may seem, our work can be therapeutic, re-creating us. What a blessing when our work is re-creation! We suffer when we are unable to work—to participate in daily activities.

Spiritual Exercise:

Make a list of the chores which you hope to do today. Pray over this list, asking God to enliven each item with an understanding of His will for you.

If you are physically handicapped and cannot work, make a list of persons you can contact by phone or remember in prayer in a special way, or to whom you can write a personal letter.

Make Me Brave

God, make me brave for life,
Oh, braver than this!
Let me straighten after pain
As a tree straightens after rain
Shining and lovely again.

God, make me brave for life,
Much braver than this!
As the blown grass lifts, let me rise
From sorrow with quiet eyes,
Knowing Thy way is wise.

God, make me brave—Life brings
Such blinding things.
Help me to keep my sight,
Help me to see aright
That out of the dark—comes light.

—*Grace Noll Crowell*[14]

24

Courage to Face Life

Moses, in his commission to Joshua, said,

"Be strong! Be courageous! Do not be afraid. . . . For the Lord your God will be with you. He will neither fail you nor forsake you" (Deuteronomy 31:6, LB).

"Be strong and take courage,
    all you whose hope is in the Lord" (Psalm 31:24, NEB).

Courage is a challenging word. It addresses us in our life's circumstances regardless of where we are at the moment. It says to us, "Face life with its hardships, its difficulties, its losses. Know that God has planned whatever comes and that His grace, working in you His good pleasure, will triumph over all adversity."

Courage challenges us to action. If we are truly "of good courage" as Moses admonished Joshua in the above quotation, our lives will shout to the world that God is triumphant over circumstances.

Benediction:

Go forth to meet the day with strong courage. Trust God to direct all circumstances of your day that you may glorify Him.

The Human Touch

'Tis the human touch in this world that counts,
    The touch of your hand and mine,
Which means far more to the fainting heart
    Than shelter and bread and wine;
For shelter is gone when the night is o'er,
    And bread lasts only a day,
But the touch of the hand and the sound of the voice
    Sing on in the soul alway.

—*Spencer Michael Free*[15]

25

Interdependence

When we find ourselves the recipients of special favors from others, we sometimes feel that it would be easier to be on the giving side than on the receiving side of life. Although we willingly say "Thank you" for favors received, we sometimes wish that we could be on the side of saying, "You're welcome." And yet we want to be gracious receivers. For bearing one another's burdens is only half of the story of Christian sharing. We must be willing to let others help us bear our burdens.

There is a beautiful word that can help us in our dilemma. It is *interdependence*. While we must depend on others, at the same time they are depending on us for a variety of favors: moral support, lessons we have learned from painful circumstances, a smile, a word of hope.

I am reminded of the story of a blind man helping a lame man to walk. The lame man, though handicapped, was able to see and thus serve as guide to his friend.

To receive the full benefit of God's love, we must pass it on to others. others. "Once you have experienced God's love, you want to pass it on."

Rather than apologizing for our leaning upon another, rather than turning aside from a proffered hand, in the spirit of interdependence, let us see what contribution we can make to others in our particular circumstances.

Spiritual Exercise:

Think of a life which you know has continued to contribute beauty to others though handicapped in some way. Ask God to use you in spite of limitations.

Day by Day

I heard a voice at evening softly say:
    Bear not thy yesterday into tomorrow,
    Nor load this week with last week's load of sorrow;
    Lift all thy burdens as they come, nor try
    To weight the present with the by and by.
One step, and then another, take thy way—
        Live day by day.

        Live day by day.
Though autumn leaves are withering round thy way,
    Walk in the sunshine. It is all for thee.
    Push straight ahead as long as thou canst see.
    Dread not the winter where thou mayst go;
    But when it comes, be thankful for the snow.
Onward and upward. Look and smile and pray—
        Live day by day.

—Julia Harris May[16]

26

A Happy Day

"Have a good day!" we are often told by our friends, perhaps as we close a telephone conversation. And what happens when we have a good day? In Micah 6:8 we are told three ways by which we can have a happy day:

> He has showed you, O man, what is good; and what does the Lord
> require of you
> but to do justice,
> and to love kindness,
> and to walk humbly with your God?

The first two have to do with our relationship with our fellowman. We are to do justice and to love kindness. As we think back on our days, we know that the happier ones were days of good relationships. As we lift the burdens of another, we find that our days of sorrow are lightened.

And, we are told that we are to walk humbly with our God. I have often wondered just what we mean when we close a friendly conversation with the greeting: "Take care!" The words of the song, "Christian Walk Carefully," come to my mind. If we are to have a happy day, we will need to walk carefully, prayerfully, avoiding the dangers and temptations of a self-absorbed day.

Again, as you face a day of ordinary living, it will be a happy one if you "do justice, love kindness, and walk humbly with your God."

Benediction:
We commit ourselves to your keeping. May all our deeds bear fruit and bring honor to your name. Make us vessels of Your grace.

I Look to Thee in Every Need

I look to Thee in every need,
And never look in vain;
I feel Thy strong and tender love,
And all is well again;
The thought of Thee is mightier far
Than sin and pain and sorrow are.

Discouraged in the work of life,
Disheartened by its load,
Shamed by its failures and its fears,
I sink beside the road;
But let me only think of Thee
And then new heart springs up in me.

Thy calmness bends serene above,
My restlessness to still;
Around me flows the quickening life,
To nerve my faltering will;
Thy presence fills my solitude,
Thy providence turns all to good.

Enfolded deep in Thy dear love,
Held in Thy law I stand;
Thy hand in all things I behold,
And all things in Thy hand;
Thou leadest me in unsought ways,
And turn'st my mourning into praise.

—*Samuel Longfellow*

27

Looking for Answers

Most of us acknowledge that we believe in the power of prayer, yet how many of us avail ourselves of the privilege of communing with the Most High God? Or we ask for blessings, promptly forgetting that we asked, and do not look for an answer.

—*Otto Unruh*

A pastor called for a meeting to pray for rain because of a drought in his community. On the way to the meeting he met a little girl carrying an umbrella. Amused, he asked the child the reason for having an umbrella. He felt ashamed when she said, "Well, we're having a prayer meeting to ask for rain."

Not only do we fail to look for answers to our prayers, but we are often surprised when the answers come.

Spiritual Exercise:

If you were to go to a prayer meeting this morning, what would you give as your greatest personal needs? Write out a list of these needs, repeating them in your prayers during this week. At the end of the week thank God for answers to these prayers. Remember that God's answer is sometimes *No*, and at other times *Wait*, so a prayer may be answered even though it may not seem so at the time.

The Wages of Love

The wages of love are small—so small
    You scarce might know they were paid at all:
The warmth of a smile, the touch of a hand—
    Coin of hearts that understand;
A name soft-whispered, a lingering kiss,
    The wages of love are paid in this;
But many a silk-clad life of ease
    Would barter its purse of gold for these.

—Author Unknown

28

Love's Tokens

It was probably a mistake to pursue happiness; much better to
create happiness; still better to create happiness for others. The
more happiness you created for others the more would be yours—
a solid satisfaction that no one could ever take away from you.

—Lloyd Douglas[17]

Probably the best way to lift ourselves from the doldrums is to see where we
can create happiness. This does not mean an empty escapism from reality but
simply filling our time by noticing the needs of others.

It is possible to be so wrapped up in our own grief that we fail to think of our
friends, who also have to bear the burdens of the day. On the other hand, we can
build mature relationships in which we are free to share our feelings and be open
to the feelings of our friends. A caring relationship is one in which there can be
mutual burden-bearing, giving us a lift as we lighten the burdens of our friends.

Spiritual Exercise:

Think through your list of close friends, being sensitive to ways in which you
can share. Is there someone among your acquaintances who is suffering from a
burden that is not easy to talk about? Can you let this person know that you truly
care by doing something tangible to show your love?

I Needed the Quiet

I needed the quiet so He drew me aside
Into the shadows where we could confide,
Away from the bustle where all the day long
I hurried and worried when active and strong.

I needed the quiet though at first I rebelled,
But gently, so gently, my cross He upheld,
And whispered so sweetly of spiritual things.
Though weakened in body, my spirit took wings
To heights never dreamed of when active and gay.
He loved me so greatly He drew me away.

I needed the quiet. No prison my bed,
But a beautiful valley of blessings instead—
A place to grow richer in Jesus to hide.
I needed the quiet so He drew me aside.

—*Alice Hansche Mortenson*[18]

29

Godliness with Contentment

An interesting story is told in 2 Samuel 19:31-39 of the aged man Barzillai who had been of special help to King David. The king offered to reward him for his kindness, but he refused, for he was content with what he had. He said, "How many years have I still to live, that I should go up with the king to Jerusalem? I am this day eighty years old; can I discern what is pleasant and what is not? Can your servant taste what he eats or what he drinks? Can I still listen to the voice of singing men and singing women? Why then should your servant be an added burden to my lord the king? . . . Why should the king recompense me with such a reward? Pray let your servant return, that I may die in my own city, near the grave of my father and my mother."

This gentleman had learned contentment in the situation in which he found himself.

What is contentment? Webster says that contentment is "the state of being satisfied with what one has." We are told in the New Testament that "there is great gain in godliness with contentment" (1 Timothy 6:6).

Perhaps it is easier to be satisfied with what we *have* than with what we *are*. Many people shortchange their attributes as they look on the talents and abilities of their friends as being superior. God has not shortchanged any of us when it comes to talents and abilities. Peter writes to "God's scattered people" that they must be "mentally stripped for action, perfectly self-controlled" (1 Peter 1:13, NEB). Paul tells Timothy, "Rekindle the gift of God that is within you" (2 Timothy 1:6). In other words, Timothy should analyze his talents and, satisfied with what God had given him, he should use his gifts for the kingdom of God.

If we are content with what we have and with what we are, we are ready to be used for God's purposes, and in this way godliness with contentment will be great gain.

Benediction:

"May the grace of the Lord Jesus Christ, and the love of God, and the fellowship of the Holy Spirit be with you all"
(2 Corinthians 13:14, NIV).

Not as a Thief

O Death, thou canst not pilfer me
    When thou shalt come, on silent wing;
When friends may mourn the lifeless clay
    And solemn are the songs they sing.

For then, O Death, I shall have wealth;
    Arrived I shall be; run, the race;
No longer tears my meat, but joy
    When I shall see my Father's face.

Then shall my faith be realized;
    Hope be my fruit, all ripe at last.
Then shall I breathe love's atmosphere,
    Pure heaven's air, eternal, vast.

There shall I quit me of all pain
    And gnawing hunger of the soul
In company of all the blest
    I shall be free of Time's harsh toll.

No, Death, thou canst not pilfer me
    When thou wilt come, some day or night;
For I shall fall asleep to wake
    To joy and everlasting light.

—*J. Paul Sauder*[19]

30

Victorious Death

For to me to live is Christ, but to die is gain.

—*Philippians 1:21*

Probably the last part of this verse depends on the first part, for if to live is Christ, to die *is* gain. It is that simple.

J. D. Charles, respected dean and teacher at Hesston College, was stricken in the midst of his active, fruitful years. It was soon evident that his illness would be terminal. A devout Christian, he faced his death in the spirit of the above affirmation of the Apostle Paul. He was granted a vision of the glories awaiting him.

Not everyone sees a vision on his deathbed, but every Christian's death can be victorious so that death shall be swallowed up in victory.

"Precious in the sight of the Lord is the death of his saints" Psalm 116:15.

Spiritual Exercise:

If you were to face your own death, what would you have to pass on? Write down the things that make up your spiritual legacy.

My Shepherd

The Lord is my shepherd;
   I have everything I need.
He lets me rest in fields of green grass
   and leads me to quiet pools of fresh water.
He gives me new strength.
He guides me in the right paths,
   as he has promised.
Even if I go through the deepest darkness,
   I will not be afraid, Lord,
   for you are with me.
Your shepherd's rod and staff protect me.

You prepare a banquet for me,
   where all my enemies can see me;
   You welcome me as an honored guest
   and fill my cup to the brim.
I know that your goodness and love will be
   with me all my life;
and your house will be my home as long as
   I live.

—Psalm 23, TEV

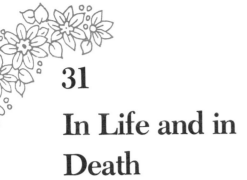

31

In Life and in Death

A minister of the gospel and head of an important church board, Howard Zehr went to his doctor and learned that he had a terminal illness and that his days were numbered.

Howard was not a stranger to death. At the age of twelve he had lost his father, and his mother died when he was twenty. Yet it was different to face death himself. However, his deep faith in God came to the surface. He was asked to share this faith in various churches, with several groups, and on a local television station. When asked whether he would like to prepare his testimony to be included in this book, he readily agreed. This is what he wrote:

It wasn't without inner struggles that I heard the verdict from my physician that my severe back pains were being caused by a tumor that could not be extracted. The various tests given indicated that it was cancer.

But there soon came to me a great and unexplainable peace of mind. The best explanation that I can give is that I am experiencing what the Scriptures speak of as the peace of God that passes all understanding. I prayed about this much. Hundreds of others prayed for me. Special prayer services have been held for me. But the pain has persisted. I feel within me as though my answer is somewhat of the kind given to the Apostle Paul when he said he prayed three times for a thorn to be removed from his flesh and then received the answer, "My grace is sufficient for you; my strength is made perfect through weakness."

This illness has helped me to understand and experience new dimensions of the lordship of Christ over my life. I realize that it is really the nature and extent of my commitment to Jesus Christ which really makes it possible for me to walk through this experience as I do. My life is committed to Jesus Christ as my Lord to the degree of my understanding of what that means and involves. I have promised Him to follow Him and to witness to Him and for Him whether by life or by death.

Recent months have opened opportunities before me which I never could have had apart from this experience. I have been asked to share my experiences and feelings with a number of groups and churches, as well as in some secular settings. I cannot share my experiences of illness without also sharing my faith, because they have become one.

Certain Scriptures have taken on new meaning for me such as, "As thy days so shall thy strength be." "Though I walk through the valley

of the shadow of death, I will fear no evil; for Thou art with me." And the one in John 8 where Jesus says, "He that believeth on me shall not see death."

Encouragement and affirmation from many of my spiritual brothers and sisters have been a tremendous resource. God be praised for the wonderful resources of His grace!

Howard did not wait until his time of *crisis* to experience God's grace. Likewise, if *we* want to be prepared for difficult experiences in life, we need to take advantage of His present-day adequacy.

Spiritual Exercise:

If you were to give *your* testimony of how God's grace is sufficient for *your* needs, how would you express this? Watch for opportunities to share this experience.

Acknowledgments

1. From *On Guard* by Joseph Sizoo (copyright 1941 by Macmillan Publishing Co., Inc., renewed 1969 by Florence Mapes Sizoo, William M. Sizoo, and Joseph M. Sizoo). Reprinted by permission.

2. Reproduced by permission, Evangelical Publishers, Toronto, Canada.

3. Reprinted by permission of Ruth Brunk Stoltzfus, Concord Associates, Harrisonburg, Va. 22801.

4. Reprinted from *Now* (Le Tourneau), Longview, Texas.

5. Reprinted from *Gospel Herald*, Scottdale, Pennsylvania, by permission of the author.

6. From *Better Than Gold* (copyright 1970 by Thomas Nelson Inc.). Reprinted by permission of the author.

7. Reprinted from the Goshen College *Bulletin*, Goshen, Indiana, by permission of Goshen College and Jill's family.

8. From *The Best Loved Poems of the American People* selected by Hazel Felleman (copyright 1936 by Doubleday & Company Inc.).

9. *Ibid.*

10. From *Poems That Touch the Heart* by A. L. Alexander (copyright 1941 by Doubleday & Company Inc.).

11. From *The Hiding Place*, © 1971 by Corrie ten Boom and John and Elizabeth Sherrill. Published by Chosen Books, Lincoln, Va. 22078. Used by permission.

12. From *Something to Live By* by Dorothea S. Kopplin (copyright 1945 by Garden City Books).

13. Reprinted from *Ideals*, Milwaukee, Wisconsin.

14. Originally titled, "A Prayer for Courage." Reprinted from *Poems of Inspiration and Courage* by Grace Noll Crowell, copyright 1930 by Harper & Row, Publishers, Inc.; renewed 1958 by Grace Noll Crowell. Reprinted by permission of the publisher.

15. From *The Best Loved Poems of the American People*, *op. cit.*

16. From *Strength for Living* by Hazel T. Wilson (copyright 1960 by Abingdon Press).

17. Quoted in *Better Than Gold*, *op. cit.*

18. From *The Christian Herald*, "The Patchwork Page," January 1977.

19. Reprinted from *Gospel Herald*, Scottdale, Pennsylvania, by permission of the author.

Born in Harrisonburg, Virginia, **Helen Good Brenneman** spent her childhood years near Hyattsville, Maryland, a suburb of Washington, D.C. She studied at Eastern Mennonite and Goshen colleges, and worked for four years as a clerk in the U.S. Department of Agriculture. Always interested in writing, Helen longed as a girl to become a newspaper reporter, but later found herself instead writing articles, stories, women's inspirational talks, and devotional books.

Following her marriage to Virgil Brenneman in 1947, the couple served a year in a refugee camp operated by the Mennonite Central Committee in Gronau, Germany, before going to Goshen, Indiana, where her husband studied for the ministry. They served for ten years in two pastorates, at Iowa City, Iowa, and Goshen, Indiana. Virgil is presently a representative for Investers Diversified Services (IDS), Inc. The Brennemans are the parents of two boys and two girls, as well as a foster daughter.

Other books by Mrs. Brenneman are *Meditations for the New Mother, But Not Forsaken, My Comforters, Meditations for the Expectant Mother, To the New Mother, The House by the Side of the Road, Ring a Dozen Doorbells, Marriage: Agony and Ecstasy,* and *Learning to Cope.*